The
Big
Flood

THE BIG FLOOD

By Wendy Pfeffer

Illustrated by Vanessa Lubach

The Millbrook Press
Brookfield, Connecticut

For Marianne, Paul, and Nagle, with special thanks to Nagle, who
convinced me that a computer would release a flood of words.—W. P.

For Lucy Brown—V. L.

Library of Congress Cataloging–in Publication Data
Pfeffer, Wendy, 1929–
The big flood / by Wendy Pfeffer ; illustrated by Vanessa Lubach.
p. cm.
ISBN 0–7613–1653–1 (lib. bdg.)
1. Floods—Mississippi River valley—Juvenile literature. [1. Floods—
Mississippi River Valley.] I. Lubach, Vanessa. II. Title.
GN1399.4.M72 P44 2001
363.34'93'097709049—dc21   00–028381

Text copyright © 2001 by Wendy Pfeffer
Illustrations copyright © 2001 by Vanessa Lubach

Published by The Millbrook Press, Inc.
2 Old New Milford Road
Brookfield, Connecticut 06804
www.millbrookpress.com

A winding river called the Mississippi wanders through fertile farm country.
    Maple and birch trees line its banks.
Bald eagles soar over the treetops
    before dipping down to snatch a catfish for dinner.
Passengers on festive riverboats
    wave to barge captains,
        and watch in wonder
            at all the farms that cover the countryside.

Patti Brandon lives on one of those farms
        with her pet goat, Molly, and her dog, Sam.
            Her family grows soybeans.
When the family's not farming,
        Patti's dad tinkers with his tractor.
Her mom keeps the books and buys supplies.
Grandpa cares for the farm animals,
        and Patti talks on her ham radio.
She calls her friends,
            tells them that Molly is going to be a mama,
                asks when the next softball game will be,
                    and chats about the rain.

Rain is important to farmers.
Too little can ruin their crops.
        Too much can flood their fields.
This summer the rain rages on,
        day after day after day.
Maple and birch trees soon stand in water.
Eagles move inland where mice and rabbits roam.
The river seems to dare fishermen to come and fish.
        But none come. Neither do the boats.
They can't maneuver the wild current.
"The river's coming up fast," Mom says, with a worried
        frown.
                "Every farm along this river could be flooded."
"It could be the worst flood in eighty years,"
        Grandpa says, eyeing the rising water.

"Patti, get on the radio," Dad says with a troubled voice.
"We need help to block the river from flooding our fields
    and our neighbors' fields."
Patti rushes to her ham radio. She calls friends and neighbors.
"The river's rising," she says breathlessly.
    "Fill dump trucks with sand! Bring empty bags!"

Patti clicks off her radio, wraps a raincoat around it,
   and lugs it through driving rain to a trailer on higher land.
Patti's mom backs out the pickup truck and heads for
   the market in town.
She stands in a long line with worried people and crying
   children to buy milk, juice, bread,
      paper plates, coffee, and doughnuts.

Outside, the rain comes down in sheets.
Neighbors arrive in rain slickers and hip boots
    as the reckless river laps at the soybean fields.
Trucks dump sand in cone-shaped piles.
Patti's neighbors work side by side.

Old Mr. Tomlin holds an empty bag
    while his son shovels heavy, wet sand into it.
Patti's softball team stacks the sacks at the water's edge
    to keep the farms from melting into mud.

Patti's mom sets up kitchen in the trailer.
She makes coffee, piles up paper plates,
    and takes time off only to glance out the trailer window,
        through the driving rain, down to the raging river.
With static crackling from the ham radio in the background,
    Patti and her friends make heaps of sandwiches,
        hurrying as if it's a race.
Patti knows the only real race is with the river.
People Patti never saw before bring barbecued pork,
    scalloped potatoes, pickled beets,
        and bottled water to the trailer.
"I couldn't feel worse if my own fields were flooding,"
    says a lady bringing in a platter of chocolate-chip cookies.
"Not only is the river flooding the fields," the lady continues,
    "but it's carrying animals along with it."
"I have to check Molly," Patti yells to her friends.
    "Someone listen for the radio."
Without being asked, the lady takes Patti's place making sandwiches.

Patti and Sam run through the driving rain into the barn.
    No Molly!
Patti sees Grandpa moving a litter of noisy hogs to higher ground.
Their frightened squeals remind Patti of how panicky Molly must be.
Patti searches the watery countryside for her pet,
    while she helps Grandpa carry grain to a flock of sheep
    stranded by spreading fingers of water.
Then she spies Molly, huddled in back of the trailer.

"You must have been here all along,"
    Patti says, reaching her pet's side.
She gives her a big hug and feels the baby inside Molly move.
As rain beats down,
    Patti ties Molly behind the trailer under a lean-to roof.

Instead of going into the warm, dry trailer,
    Patti and Sam hurry down to the water's edge.
Grandma Higgens from next door directs the dump trucks,
    while her three sons, Nathan, Jacob, and Joseph, work the pumps.
But the water drenches the land
    faster than the pumps can drain it.
Patti pinches herself to see if this is all just a nasty nightmare.
It isn't. So Patti joins the group shoveling sand.
The river rushes on
    carrying with it chicken coops, sofas, and memories.
A family photo album
    and a blue ribbon won at the state fair float by.

Midnight comes.
Flashlights sweep back and forth searching for leaks between
    sandbags.
Lightning flashes and thunder rolls in from the west...then
    comes more rain.
Patti shivers in the cold, damp air. Sam nuzzles her leg.
"Will this rain ever stop?" Patti asks Sam.

When daylight breaks, Patti carries coffee and doughnuts to
          waterlogged workers.
The river rushes along carrying anything in its path:
          picnic tables, trees, henhouses, rabbit hutches.
Half submerged in whitecaps,
          a ragged teddy bear seems to be calling for help as it's
                    carried downstream.
Patti thinks of her own teddy bear, her house, her family, Molly, and Sam.
          Will they stay safe?
She feels worried and wants to cry.
But Patti has no time for tears.
She goes into the trailer
          and hears a call for help come over her radio.
"Worker slipped...raging waters...barely see him."

Switching to another channel,
Patti tries to control the trembling in her voice as she
calls a helicopter.
She runs to the window and sees the worker.
Noisy helicopter blades whirl overhead.
Patti sees a rope going down from the helicopter...
hands appearing out of the swirling foam...
fingers clutching at the line...
"They got him," a voice yells. "It's my Jacob," calls
Grandma Higgens.
Patti takes a deep breath, grateful that Jacob is okay.
As the helicopter heads for high, dry land
with Jacob dangling from the rope,
Nathan yells, "We're lucky Patti was at the radio."
The workers cheer, and Patti goes back to her radio
as the drenched, soggy, tired workers toil on.

Finally the angry rain clouds blow away,
    and the muddy waters flow more slowly.
The river, which once roared like a lion,
    now laps at the sandbags like a pussycat.
Neighbors and families hug and cheer
    as the river slips slowly back into its bed.
Patti switches off her radio, calls Sam,
    and trudges through mud to her waterlogged house.
She pulls back her soggy bedspread
    and finds a dead catfish, two frogs, and *worms*...
        long, wiggly night crawlers, wiggling everywhere.
"Yuck!" yells Patti, and quickly covers them.
She thinks she might be sick.
"There's so much to do," says Patti's mom, taking a deep breath.
"Let's get to work," says Dad,
    still bleary-eyed from having no sleep.

Sloshing through a world that looks like chocolate pudding
    but smells like dead rats,
        Patti and her family shovel mud and muck
            from every corner of their house until it's livable.
And they're still not done!
For days they clear away barrels and driftwood,
    dump sand back into trucks,
        return missing animals to neighbors,
            and build a new house for Sam.
After weeks of exhausting work,
    farm life along the river returns almost to normal.

Patti calls her friends,
        tells them what a good mama Molly is,
                asks them if they know the lady who brought the cookies,
                        and worries with them on rainy days.
On sunny days Patti and Sam eat lunch
        under a maple tree along the river,
                happy that it's flowing along like it used to.
She watches the bald eagles soar overhead,
        before they dip down to snatch catfish.
Passengers on festive riverboats and captains on long barges
        wave to Patti as they glide by.
She waves back and watches the winding river
        wander through fertile farm country
                as if nothing ever happened.

This story is based on the Big Flood of 1993 in the upper midwestern region of the United States. The flood occurred after the soaking rainfall of the previous autumn, heavy snowmelt of spring, and drenching rain of summer filled the streams and rivers leading into the Mississippi River.

The damage from this, the biggest flood in the history of the United States, cost about $17,000,000,000 (17 billion dollars).

The flooding waters spread over 23 million acres (9 million hectares). That's bigger than the whole state of Texas.

In Missouri a family went back to their home by boat and swam through the front door.

In Des Moines, Iowa, postal workers hung up 30,000 pieces of mail to dry in a garage.

Everywhere they looked there was water, but for twelve days 250,000 people in Des Moines had no water to drink, shower, or flush toilets.

Earthen dams called levees had been built all along the river to hold back flooding waters. But the river made these powerless by going over them, under them, and right through them by way of animal burrows and plant roots.

At the flood's highest point, almost 8 million gallons (30 million liters) of water raced past the city of St. Louis, Missouri, each second. That's eleven times faster than water flows over Niagara Falls.

Years ago wetlands bordered the Mississippi River on both sides. These bordering floodplains acted as a giant sponge when the river overflowed. Plants in the floodplains also stopped the flow of flooding water. When levees and dams were built, people didn't see the need for floodplains anymore, so they bought the land next to the river, built homes, and farmed the fertile soil. When the floods came, the giant sponge was gone. Plants no longer stopped the water's flow. If the land bordering the river were to become floodplains again, future floods might not be as devastating as the Big Flood of 1993.